When a Seed Grows

Poetry by

DE'SHAWN MAURICE

Copyright © 2018 De'Shawn Maurice

All rights reserved.

ISBN-13: 978-1-7286-2910-0

To anyone who may need this.

CONTENTS

the Seed (Introduction)   1

the Germination (Our Innocence)   3

the Sprouting (Our Vulnerabilities)   40

the Flowering (Our Growth)   63

the Reproduction (Our Strength)   101

the Seed (Introduction)

When a Seed Grows

A seed is planted with the objective to grow. In the process that flower can be overlooked. Unappreciated of its beauty. Stepped on without a care. Environmental stress causing damage to its growth. And after all that, somehow they still blossom into something that the world relies on for comfort through good and bad times. Just like a seed is how our life is. We're planted on this earth. Going through a lot of similar things but not shared or seen on the surface by one another. In the end though, we'll blossom despite how slow the process may feel. I present to you the similarities I've gone through with my poetry in hopes that you know you're not alone

De'Shawn Maurice

the Germination (Our Innocence)

When a Seed Grows

You were beautiful
before I tried to convince you.
If nothing else,
I want you to see your potential.

De'Shawn Maurice

You did your part,
you kind soul.
People will stay
only when they want.

When a Seed Grows

All I wanted
was to show you who I am
and for you to be impressed.
You'll remember my face
but not the heart I had
waiting behind my chest.

De'Shawn Maurice

Let yourself glow,
and you'll see the hate shine bright, too.
Let yourself fail,
and they'll love that you're right there
with them, too.

When a Seed Grows

Why judge people
on how they live their life,
like it has anything to do with you?
It's their life.
Mind your business and be nice.

De'Shawn Maurice

Everyone dances to their own beat.
Moves through life at their own pace.
Social media makes us think
we're all in a race.

There's reasons why our objectives don't always
play out how we imagined.
Yes, visualizing is important. But not all things
are for us to have.

De'Shawn Maurice

Never understood the accuracy
on a compass rose.
Still don't know where my life
is supposed to go.

When a Seed Grows

You want to spend so much time
in the company of others,
but when's the last time
you found pleasure with just yourself?

De'Shawn Maurice

Even the most beautiful islands are
forced to be isolated from the world.

When a Seed Grows

A relationship with yourself
is much needed.
Everyone has an agenda
you don't see coming.
Be your bestest friend till the end.

De'Shawn Maurice

No matter what you're feeling,
embrace it.
You gotta go through it
to understand it.

When a Seed Grows

We don't know until we try.
And if we can walk away giving it the best we had, there's no reason to let them see us cry.

De'Shawn Maurice

Told myself, go on - take a risk. You got one lifetime to make the most of it.

When a Seed Grows

Going back in time
would be safer
than an unknown future.
I held on not allowing
what's next to come to me.

De'Shawn Maurice

The beautiful thing about flying
is going places you never been.
Not only exploring the city
but learning about yourself from within.

When a Seed Grows

Time is treated like it's unlimited for us.

Like it can come back.

Focus on what matters;

not what we lack.

De'Shawn Maurice

I painted the perfect picture
of who I thought you were.
You showed me your true colors
now the art is a blur.

When a Seed Grows

"Trust me" is my favorite lie.

De'Shawn Maurice

I was too scared to let you go.
Afraid I couldn't find better
until I looked deeply at myself.

When a Seed Grows

It isn't Love I lack
because I give it
even when it's not reciprocated.
It's the Strength I seek
because I lose myself
in the midst of loving others.

De'Shawn Maurice

May our efforts be in our favor,
for our will was tested not to.

When a Seed Grows

People value new gifts
no matter if they asked.
The lesson here is
if they wanted to take advantage
of your presence,
they would have.

De'Shawn Maurice

What are the chances
things will fall through?
I don't know
but I'm willing to travel
down that road with you.

When a Seed Grows

Took a few shots
trying dating and whatnot.
Left me more to myself
split between the haves and have-nots.

De'Shawn Maurice

I've asked myself,

what's stopping my growth?

Why am I still not there?

Then I looked around

and realized I never moved from here.

When a Seed Grows

We give people chance after chance,
like it's in our DNA.
In denial thinking they'd change,
all because we want what's
not healthy to stay.

De'Shawn Maurice

You know what you have to do.
The only reason you say "I don't know"
is because you're hiding what
you don't want to do.
You're not losing the other person.
You're losing sight of you.

When a Seed Grows

Your overthinking is being in denial
of what you know to be true.
We use our thoughts to stall
on what action to do.

De'Shawn Maurice

The signs are there,
and although I read them,
I still mislead myself trying to chase you.

When a Seed Grows

It's not really your fault
when you think it is.
Your compassion isn't for
everyone you want to give it to.
- People suck

De'Shawn Maurice

I want to show you who I am
and not the assumption of who I'm not.
You don't win the jackpot if you
don't dare to match up in slots.

When a Seed Grows

What's effortless should come easy.
I made a mistake.
Thought if I reeled hard enough,
you'd take the bait.

De'Shawn Maurice

Sometimes I wish I could freeze time
so I can cherish the moment just a little
longer. Especially in times spent with you,
because I never want it to end.

When a Seed Grows

Your flaws are nonexistent with me.
I see you as a gift.
When I compliment you,
I am enlightening your value;
a spiritual uplift.

De'Shawn Maurice

...and I hope I never disappoint you.

Which I probably will.

My faults are what I'm still working on.

When a Seed Grows

the Sprouting (Our Vulnerabilities)

De'Shawn Maurice

Well, this sucks.

- Crushing on someone

When a Seed Grows

My vibe is chilled.
I'd appreciate you
not entering my realm.

De'Shawn Maurice

You play me like a new song
that gets old quickly.
That's what it means when you get
what you want and then ditch me.

When a Seed Grows

From a distance, it's easy to want what you
can't physically see.
Double tap my picture.
Like a great status.
Retweet a tweet.
But if I gave you the opportunity
you'd look right past me.

De'Shawn Maurice

I reached for your hand to help you up
because I felt you needed me.
Instead, you pulled me down.
Now I'm on the ground like I once saw you.
Hoping you're around.
That's me feeling like I need you.

Communication = works both ways

Working both ways = Me, always

De'Shawn Maurice

You tell a lie
like it's going to make me
feel any better.
I'd rather you've told the truth
so I could've walked away sooner.

When a Seed Grows

Time flies, they told me.
Faster than I prepared myself for.
I am an adult who wasn't ready.

De'Shawn Maurice

Self-pleasure is another way to cum.
Don't waste your sexual desires
on someone who will make you feel numb.

When a Seed Grows

Don't know what this is,
but it's cool.
I like you.

De'Shawn Maurice

I want to face my fears with you.
Dare me to.

When a Seed Grows

Stressing over
who don't appreciate me,
like the ones who do don't matter.
Maybe that's why
the ones who do,
call me stupid.

De'Shawn Maurice

"I love you"
is what I say in my head repeatedly.
You have no idea what you mean to me.

When a Seed Grows

A trigger of emotion happens
whenever you're in my presence.
I prefer you stay there
because I get a glimpse of heaven.

De'Shawn Maurice

I want to get lost in your mind.
Explore your thoughts.
Caress every bit of your skin
to know what gives you goosebumps.

When a Seed Grows

Caution sign before I took my step.
Knew the trouble that awaited me.
Why do we like disappointing ourselves
and blaming other's behavior?

I wonder.

De'Shawn Maurice

An old song
can leave me in a time
when I first heard it.
The older I become,
the more appreciative
I am of moments.

When a Seed Grows

I am filled with nostalgia
of the days I miss.
Excuse me if sometimes
I like to reminisce.

De'Shawn Maurice

There's times where I worry
about tomorrow when I didn't even
pay attention to today.
Over analyzing situations,
making a mess mentally
when I'm not even physically there yet.

When a Seed Grows

You automatically became a part of my past once I met you.
Signs I deny admitting say you're not meant to be in my future.
But silly me presently tries to anyway.

De'Shawn Maurice

"Let it go" is the right advice.
But I don't want to right now.
I want to believe there's still a chance
if you're still around.

August 4th

That night was everything to me.
I'll never forget.
We shared each other's souls
and it was magic.
Sometimes I wish I could relive it
but not for what we did.
To be in that feeling of blissfulness I was in.
It's a new day
and that night is far in our rear view.
For what it's worth,
I wish it was me that was still with you.

De'Shawn Maurice

the Flowering (Our Growth)

When a Seed Grows

Life isn't easy.
Life isn't fair.
But that doesn't mean you give up.
It's just testing you, dear.

De'Shawn Maurice

You ask for one thing
and receive another.
The universe is telling you
it will send you something better.

When a Seed Grows

Your downs are
just as important as your ups.
You won't learn everything
if you only fall once.

De'Shawn Maurice

Smile anyway.
You & I are still alive.

When a Seed Grows

The best way to return the favor to God is to live out your dreams the way he intended you to.

De'Shawn Maurice

I believe trusting your gut is
(G)od's (U)sage of (T)alking to us.
Believe and do your best the more he'll discuss.

When a Seed Grows

What God placed before us
isn't misleading.
We get the wrong idea
and stop believing.

De'Shawn Maurice

You have purpose.
The moment you stop
thinking you don't
is the moment you
fail to realize your value.

Absolutely everything happens for a reason.
Being honest about situations, we can live with
that truth.

De'Shawn Maurice

Traveling brings humbleness.
You see life from a different view.
Open mindedness leads you
to something new.

When a Seed Grows

A culture shock

gets you out of your comfort zone.

Makes you realize

how we all have a special home.

De'Shawn Maurice

It's not a lie
if telling you my truth
isn't your business.

When a Seed Grows

Lying because you'd feel bad
is hurting the person worse.
You choose to protect your "innocence"
than to free someone of their intuition.

De'Shawn Maurice

As much as we want to dissect things,
when we're honest to ourselves
about a situation, the answer comes.

When a Seed Grows

Lie to me once,

maybe by habit you didn't mean to.

Lie to me twice,

I assumed you were scared of truth.

Lie to me the third time,

is where I remove you.

De'Shawn Maurice

Your words are inconsistent.
No one wants to listen to someone
with a sour taste leaving their mouth.

When a Seed Grows

Put my energy into things that didn't deserve my aura.
Had to step back and regain myself.
My definition of closure.

De'Shawn Maurice

Toxic people
aren't hard to distinguish.
You'll notice the spiritual growth
once they vanish.

When a Seed Grows

Negativity can wear off you
so I stand cautious.
Society with their stupid rules
explains why I'm standoffish.

De'Shawn Maurice

Placing my energy into a safe haven
you can't touch.
Tired of people's bullshit;
I don't want to open it up.

When a Seed Grows

The lack of people's effort
should mean detachment
on your end.

De'Shawn Maurice

One must not give all

till you receive duplicate energy.

Same goes for sex.

Perfect pleasure is caused by your synergy.

When a Seed Grows

A team wins championships.
Solo players only get recognition.
What would you rather have?
Because by my side, we'd be a dynasty.
I got you, you got me.
If not, that's okay.
I can't force what don't want to stay.

De'Shawn Maurice

Time won't stop;
and we sit around,
wasting the time we're given.
Long as we're breathing,
we have a reason.

When a Seed Grows

Two things we can't get back is
our life and time.
To not take advantage of both
should be a crime.

De'Shawn Maurice

We grow up thinking
someone will make us happier.
Make us feel more alive.
10% of that can be true
but 90% of the time,
no one got you like you.

When a Seed Grows

Feeling lonely comes from
seeing people happy
with their significant other.
What you don't see is how
happy they are within
themselves to become a better lover.

De'Shawn Maurice

Channeled my attention
on what I needed to see and
not how I imagined things to be.
There's no manifestation
when you're confused about a situation.

When a Seed Grows

You can give someone
the map to happiness,
and they still wouldn't acknowledge
you pointed them in that direction.

De'Shawn Maurice

To expose yourself is 50/50.

People can see your value and leave you anyway.

When a Seed Grows

Dwelling over you won't help me one bit.
We had a "thing" now it's time I get past it.

De'Shawn Maurice

Women are the strongest creatures.
It's hidden in misunderstood features
but they're our best teachers.

When a Seed Grows

It wasn't meant to be.
What is, deserves my gratitude,
not my unhealthy attitude.

De'Shawn Maurice

People will play games with you.
There's 168 hours in a week.
You put in the effort to see them
while they hide and you seek.

When a Seed Grows

Faking my amnesia
to forget about what was.
I lost interest in who you are
and everything above.

De'Shawn Maurice

If I cut off ties
I've realized it
doesn't go well with my fit.
That's a metaphor for my life.
You don't keep around
what doesn't benefit.

When a Seed Grows

The more you're out of my sight
the more you're out of my mind.
Which is perfect.
Because since then, I've been fine.

De'Shawn Maurice

the Reproduction (Our Strength)

When a Seed Grows

The mirror told me who's in charge.

De'Shawn Maurice

My dream is
to go after my dreams.
If I don't,
I've failed the potential me
that won't ever exist.

When a Seed Grows

Obstacles are inevitable.
No fear knowing I am capable.

De'Shawn Maurice

My future
is all of what
I choose to do today.
Reminding myself
to not let anyone
get in the way.

When a Seed Grows

Fear told me I couldn't.
The universe told me I could.
The outcome left me still breathing.
Meaning things work out as they should.

De'Shawn Maurice

Are you really all that thankful for life
if you cry over irrelevant material?
What's for us stays.
What's not, fades.
And we cry
because we don't want to say goodbye.
When truthfully,
it's not supposed to bring us down
if we're looking for an up.
Everything and everyone
isn't meant for us.

When a Seed Grows

Opinions
of myself
only matter
if I choose to
believe them.

De'Shawn Maurice

Sailing is the key.
Time heals all
once we let go
and allow the motion of life
to steer us where we need to be.

When a Seed Grows

If we matched each other's effort,
the beauty would be in the results.
But it's only one sided;
I had to move on due to your faults.

De'Shawn Maurice

The source of my happiness comes
from within - my inner peace.
Your intentions could mean well
but know you can't make me happier
than I can for me.

When a Seed Grows

You are you
and you are your truth.
Somebody is going to
appreciate every bit of you.

De'Shawn Maurice

You stay where home is.
But you live to travel anywhere.

When a Seed Grows

To be stagnant is to sit.

To see the world,

you must take risks.

De'Shawn Maurice

Sky's the limit
and maybe even beyond that.
We take flight to experience
other ways of life
we don't see where we're at.

When a Seed Grows

Trying to live a little
and see the world before I die
and the world no longer sees me.

De'Shawn Maurice

You want them.

They disengage themselves.

Good news is,

you were meant for somebody else.

When a Seed Grows

HE already mapped out my destiny.
My next step is to walk faithfully.

De'Shawn Maurice

What I thought was for me
was just my greediness.
Life reminds me
the most important thing
is my happiness.

When a Seed Grows

Took everything I had
and moved away.
Didn't think twice about it.
Just knew I had to Pray.
What led me to where I am in my life
was because I made a God-willing decision.
He gives us guidance if we listen.
Pay attention.

De'Shawn Maurice

My destination won't
be smooth sailing.
It comes with distractions
by things that won't
matter after I reach it.

When a Seed Grows

Try me.

I live to be reborn again.

De'Shawn Maurice

The lesson was learned
once I got peace.

When a Seed Grows

This may hurt me in the end,
this thing between us.
Life has a way of separating things.
I won't hold it against you.

De'Shawn Maurice

No longer disappointed
in your broken words.
I shrug them off.

I'm jaded.

When a Seed Grows

We were given wings
to fly through life.
It starts with our spirit;
to uplift us and take flight.

De'Shawn Maurice

The amount of outcomes that can occur
is what scares the attempt.
But you either excel
or learn the lesson from it.

When a Seed Grows

My team when I win.

My support when I lose.

My guidance when I don't know what to do.

My honesty when I've been lied to.

I am so happy to have you.

- Friends

De'Shawn Maurice

There's not a time

you'd see me pretending to be perfect.

I'm the best of the worst thing.

People look pass me

and I make mistakes.

But there's quality waiting

for the one who acknowledges what I'm made of.

Thanks for reading.

Love, D.M.

Made in the USA
Middletown, DE
31 October 2018